I HATE ALONE

Ellen Brammar

I HATE ALONE

OBERON BOOKS
LONDON

First published in 2017 by Oberon Books Ltd
521 Caledonian Road, London N7 9RH
Tel: +44 (0) 20 7607 3637 / Fax: +44 (0) 20 7607 3629
e-mail: info@oberonbooks.com
www.oberonbooks.com

A catalogue record for this book is available from the British Library.

PB ISBN: 9781786823649
E ISBN: 9781786823656

Cover image: Josh Moore

For Claire

Production Team

Written by Ellen Brammar

Music by James Frewer

Directed by Paul Smith

Production Managed and Produced by Mungo Beaumont

Design by Natalie Young

Communications Manager – Jamie Potter

TSM – Mat Oliphant

General Manager – Emily Anderton

Middle Child Company Members

Mungo Beaumont

Ellen Brammar

Emma Bright

Sophie Clay

Edward Cole

Marc Graham

Matthew May

Paul Smith

James Stanyer

Notes

Any local references can be changed to reflect the place the play is being performed. The actors should feel free to introduce the songs. A '/' indicates an interruption.

Characters

Danielle   Larner Wallace-Taylor

Chloe   Rachel Barnes

Stephanie/Jamie/Mr. Sumner to be played by the actor playing Chloe.

Man to be played by the actor playing Danielle.

SCENE 1

CHLOE enters dragging a heavy, full bin bag with her. She softly sings as she places the bag out of the way.

CHLOE.   If I could glue myself to you, I would
          I'd pritt stick us together, if I could
          As close as can be, nose to nose
          All fingers touching and our toes

CHLOE looks at the bag for a moment. Then shyly looks at the audience.

CHLOE. Hi.

Beat.

Chloe.

Beat.

Hello.

Pause.

Hi, hello, I'm Chloe and this is a – is a – thing – this is a special thing, yeah, this is my – our special thing about us and you can watch and learn – no, you probably won't learn. This is just a thing about me / and

DANIELLE enters.

DANIELLE. Hi.

CHLOE. Hi.

DANIELLE. I'm Danielle and this is / Chloe.

CHLOE. Chloe. Yeah, I've done that bit.

DANIELLE. Oh, right. How'd it go?

CHLOE. Wonderfully.

DANIELLE. I love you. *(Beat.)* Me and Chloe have been best /

CHLOE. friends since we were four. I love you too.

DANIELLE. So, there is nothing /

CHLOE. And no one /

DANIELLE. And nothing /

CHLOE. And no one /

DANIELLE. And nothing /

CHLOE. And no one /

DANIELLE. That can change that.

CHLOE. There's no one like us.

DANIELLE. We are unique.

CHLOE. Special.

DANIELLE. Special because we have each other and always will.

CHLOE. It starts…how far should I go back?

DANIELLE. To when we first met.

CHLOE. Really?

DANIELLE. Yeah.

CHLOE. It starts, twenty-four years, three weeks, two days and seven hours ago.

DANIELLE. Impressive.

CHLOE. Thanks.

DANIELLE. In a primary school playground.

CHLOE. On the hopscotch.

DANIELLE. With Chloe lying face-down, spread eagle on the concrete. *(Beat.)* Get on the floor.

CHLOE. It's sticky.

A look from DANIELLE and CHLOE lies on the floor face-down, spread eagle.

DANIELLE. The bigger boys football soars through the air, smashing into her perfect little face and sending her flying.

CHLOE. No one notices, other than Danielle.

DANIELLE. Her little lips are all red and puffy.

CHLOE. Our little hands find each other.

DANIELLE. Little fingers all entwined.

CHLOE. Safe and secure.

DANIELLE. I pull her up /

CHLOE. And she hugs me tighter than tighter than tight.

DANIELLE. It's instant.

CHLOE. We're sure of that.

DANIELLE. Do you want to be my best friend?

CHLOE. I do.

DANIELLE. From that point on – we're inseparable.

CHLOE. We don't need anyone else.

DANIELLE. Other kids bore us.

CHLOE. They don't get our games, how to play properly.

DANIELLE. We're eight and things go a bit – pooey, for a few years.

CHLOE. But we should tell them about that later, right?

DANIELLE. Yeah. The only thing that matters now is that when we're fourteen we're best friends again.

CHLOE. Stronger than ever.

DANIELLE. And we start a band.

CHLOE. Just the two of us, no one else gets it.

DANIELLE. They don't know how to play properly.

CHLOE. Our band's called, Disabled Barbie.

DANIELLE. Chloe used to pull the legs off her Barbies.

CHLOE. Not to be mean.

DANIELLE. You were creating a more diverse community, right Chlo?

CHLOE. They wouldn't sell me a Barbie in a wheelchair.

DANIELLE. The first song we ever write is during Mr. Clayton's maths lesson.

CHLOE. It's called Maths Teacher's Bulge.

<u>Maths Teacher's Bulge</u>

Pythagoras, you tempt me
Hypotenuse you minx
Con, Sin, Tan, you trollops
Acute angle? Why yes me thinks

The maths teacher's bulge is brewing
It lies quiet and dormant no more
It's awoken by numbers and figures
Especially my figure, I'm sure

DANIELLE. This whole thing started because of Disabled Barbie.

CHLOE. Our band is special.

DANIELLE. It means everything to us.

CHLOE. Everything.

DANIELLE. So, thirty-two hours ago when Stephanie /

CHLOE. Stephanie, from 'cunts 'r' us records' /

DANIELLE. Came waddling /

CHLOE. She's heavily pregnant /

DANIELLE. Into her office /

CHLOE. Where we're waiting /

DANIELLE. So excited, 'cos this is it, we've been waiting for this for years.

CHLOE. Since we were fourteen.

DANIELLE. It's been leading to this moment, this second.

CHLOE. Our lives are about to change.

DANIELLE. We can hardly breathe.

CHLOE. This is it.

DANIELLE. This is our moment, our chance to be heard.

CHLOE. No more being ignored.

DANIELLE. People will listen and love us /

CHLOE. And worship us.

DANIELLE. Envy us.

CHLOE. Want to have sex with us.

DANIELLE. And we can't breathe /

CHLOE. 'Cos she's looking up at us from under her professionally extended lashes /

DANIELLE. And she's opening her mouth so we can glimpse those professionally whitened gnashers /

CHLOE. And this is /

DANIELLE. Fucking /

CHLOE. It /

DANIELLE. And…

CHLOE. 'No.'

DANIELLE. No?

CHLOE. 'No.'

DANIELLE. 'No, we won't sign you.'

CHLOE. Just – 'no.'

DANIELLE. But /

CHLOE. 'No.'

DANIELLE. Can we just /

CHLOE. 'No.'

DANIELLE. Just give us a chance…please.

CHLOE. 'Nope.'

DANIELLE. For fuck sake, this isn't fair.

CHLOE. 'Girls. Girls, girls, girls.'

DANIELLE. 'Let me give you some advice.'

CHLOE. 'Lower your expectations.'

DANIELLE. 'You're not ready.'

CHLOE. 'You're not there.'

DANIELLE. 'Maybe just – play for fun.'

CHLOE. 'And next time don't just barge into someone's office expecting a meeting.'

DANIELLE. 'It's not the done thing.'

CHLOE. But you wouldn't've seen us if we didn't.

DANIELLE. That's not fair.

CHLOE. 'I'm sorry, but sometimes life isn't fair.'

Beat.

DANIELLE. Fuck.

CHLOE. We were disappointed.

DANIELLE. Chloe, we were more than disappointed.

CHLOE. Right, yeah, sorry.

DANIELLE. Fuck.

CHLOE. Breathe.

DANIELLE. Fuck.

CHLOE. Take a deep breath.

DANIELLE. Fuck.

CHLOE. In, two, three / four and…

DANIELLE. Shut up.

CHLOE. I'm trying to help.

DANIELLE. Fuck them, fuck her.

CHLOE. Yeah.

DANIELLE. I just don't – this was supposed to be it and she just – just, no.

CHLOE. Breathe, Dan. Breathe.

DANIELLE. Stop telling me to breathe, Chloe.

CHLOE. It's okay, we'll – we'll try again. Yeah?

DANIELLE. What's the point? Everyone's the same, no one gets it.

CHLOE. I get it.

DANIELLE. Course this happened, when has anything ever gone right for us, ever. Our lives are shit.

CHLOE. No.

DANIELLE. Yes. Our lives are a pile of shit, one fucking disappointment after the other.

CHLOE. Not true, you have me.

DANIELLE. Yeah, I know but – that's not it. Nothing ever goes to plan for us, ever. Just think, every time something has gone wrong for us, every time something's been taken away from us, there's been someone behind it. Maybe not always really obvious, but they're there, lurking. People make other people's lives shit.

CHLOE. Stephanie?

DANIELLE. Yeah. She is just another fucker in a fucking long line of fuckers just fucking it up for us. We deserve so much more than what we have. It's not fair.

Beat.

CHLOE. And then you had a plan, didn't you Dan?

DANIELLE. Yeah. Then I had a plan.

Beat.

DANIELLE. Chloe?

CHLOE. Yeah?

DANIELLE. If I asked you to do something with / me…

CHLOE. Yep.

DANIELLE. It might get us in trouble.

CHLOE. Big trouble?

DANIELLE. Medium.

CHLOE. Nice.

DANIELLE. I want us to make a list.

CHLOE. Right.

DANIELLE. Of everyone that's fucked us over, anyone that's stopped us getting what is rightfully ours. All the fuckers that fucked it for us.

CHLOE. Yeah.

DANIELLE. And then I want us to work our way through the list and…

CHLOE. And?

DANIELLE. And take revenge.

CHLOE. Like – violent?

DANIELLE. No, not – maybe, I dunno, I – does it matter if it is? Maybe we need a bit of violence in our lives, maybe the only way to get control is to shove that other cunt out the way. I'm so tired of people making me feel weak, sometimes I just think, if I could – if I could smash their head against the wall a couple of times then they'd stop. They sure as fuck wouldn't push in front of me in a queue, or make me walk in the road as they shove past me in the street or say no to us. Would they? 'Cos they'd know what I can do, they'd know what I was capable of.

Beat.

CHLOE. So that's what we did. This is the story of that.

DANIELLE. The story of two women /

CHLOE. Best friends.

DANIELLE. Who take revenge /

CHLOE. On anyone that's wronged them.

DANIELLE. Which turns out to be a lot of people.

CHLOE. Two women filled with hate.

DANIELLE. But it wasn't their fault.

CHLOE. Nope.

DANIELLE. They just wanted their lives to be something special.

CHLOE. Because we all deserve that.

DANIELLE. Remember that, as you stand there.

CHLOE. Please.

DANIELLE. And we'll try to remember to tell you the truth.

I Hate Them

DANIELLE: My flat is small
CHLOE: My Mum doesn't know me
DANIELLE: I can't afford a holiday
CHLOE: My girlfriends leave me
DANIELLE: She gets paid more than me
CHLOE: He's successful and fit

We want to be envied
We want to be unique
Everyone is boring
Everyone is dull
We hate them

We're sluts
We're freaks
We're bossy
We're weak
We're forgotten
We're ignored
We're downtrodden
And we're bored

We were supposed to be treasured
An unbelievable success
A triumph of sperm and ovum
To be envied and adored
To make people hate themselves just a little bit more
You fucked it for us
Fucked it for us

We need to be envied
We need to be unique
Everyone to love me
Everyone to loathe me
We hate them
We hate them

SCENE 2

CHLOE. If you fuck us, we'll fuck you.

DANIELLE. If you've ever fucked us over, you better watch out.

CHLOE. Chloe and Danielle are coming for you.

DANIELLE. We know where you live.

CHLOE. We know what you did.

DANIELLE. You can't run.

CHLOE. You can't hide.

DANIELLE. We will find you.

CHLOE. This is so much fun.

DANIELLE. Okay, right, so, okay – list.

CHLOE. Shit, there's a lot of people to get through. I feel a bit tired.

DANIELLE. Do you want me to schedule in a nap?

CHLOE. Yeah.

DANIELLE. I was joking you great big sausage.

CHLOE. I know.

DANIELLE. Sure.

CHLOE. Should we just – crack on?

DANIELLE. Yeah, s'pose so. Stephanie?

CHLOE. Might as well, we're still standing outside her office.

DANIELLE. Okay, great.

CHLOE. Just barge in?

DANIELLE. Yep.

CHLOE. Yep.

DANIELLE. Ready?

CHLOE. Yep.

DANIELLE. Okay. We power walk back to the revolving door, wiggly bums speed into the lift and ping, up to the fourth floor. Storming our way into reception we demand to see Stephanie.

CHLOE. Stephanie!

DANIELLE. *(As if to receptionist.)* No, we don't – we were literally just here.

CHLOE. *(To receptionist.)* No, we won't.

BOTH. Stephanie!

DANIELLE. She hears us, we're making a right racket, and out she struts, slash, waddles from her plush glass cube, like a shitter.

STEPHANIE. Girls?

DANIELLE. Fuck you, Stephanie.

STEPHANIE. Danielle.

DANIELLE. This is absolute bullshit.

STEPHANIE. Danielle.

DANIELLE. You just can't bear it that we might be more successful than you. You're jealous.

STEPHANIE. Danielle.

DANIELLE. You think you're so much better than us 'cos you get to work in a cunty glass cube, and live in Leeds.

STEPHANIE. Danielle.

DANIELLE. Stop saying my name, Stephanie.

STEPHANIE. I understand this is probably a bit hard for you, but we've made our decision.

DANIELLE. We would have been brilliant, Stephanie, you wouldn't know talent if it pissed on your face.

STEPHANIE. Actually, Danielle, I would. I know talent, I see talent all the time. You aren't talent. You don't have it. We're not going to sign you, like I said, like I can keep saying if you want me to? You're not – marketable. For goodness sake girls, you're called 'Disabled Barbie'.

DANIELLE. Yeah?

CHLOE. They wouldn't sell me one in a wheelchair.

DANIELLE. It's a good name. It's socially aware.

STEPHANIE. No, it's not. Look, girls, I understand you're disappointed but you need to calm down. You're embarrassing yourselves.

DANIELLE. What?

STEPHANIE. It's getting a bit embarrassing.

Beat.

DANIELLE. This is the point where I snap. Right here.

STEPHANIE. It's getting a bit embarrassing.

DANIELLE. See.

STEPHANIE. A bit embarrassing.

DANIELLE. There.

STEPHANIE. Embarrassing.

DANIELLE. And I have all these really dark thoughts. Like dark dark. Like…

CHLOE. No one here's gonna judge you, Dan. Right? Best to just say it.

DANIELLE. Thanks Chlo, thanks everyone. Like – like shoving her to the floor and stamping right on her tummy and then – and then she sort of erupts with blood, like John Hurt in *Alien*, and this gross blood-covered baby crawls out and looks up at me and says, 'I can't stand being inside this cunt any longer, will you be my mum instead?' And I pick the little monster up and we both watch as Stephanie lies bleeding to death at our feet. *(Pause.)* I don't do that though, I'm not a complete heartless bitch, I just – I thought it, that's all. In that moment /

STEPHANIE. A bit embarrassing.

DANIELLE. I just wanted her to feel some fucking pain.

CHLOE. Understandable.

DANIELLE. Thanks Chlo, thanks everyone. This next bit though – this bit I did. So, she goes /

STEPHANIE. It's getting a bit embarrassing.

DANIELLE. Embarrassing?

STEPHANIE. Yes, embarrassing. You are embarrassing yourselves.

DANIELLE. Fuck you.

DANIELLE snaps, she pulls down her jeans, whips off her knickers, kicks off her Adidas, runs into STEPHANIE's cunty glass cube, and climbs up onto her desk.

CHLOE. Jeans, knickers, Adidas – off.

DANIELLE. Fucking embarrassing.

STEPHANIE. Don't you dare. Danielle this is ridicu – Get out of my cunty glass – oops, sorry – get out my office. Get off my desk, I have contracts – are you going to? You are so fucking weird. Get down now.

DANIELLE. Piss. Pissy, piss, piss, piss.

STEPHANIE. You're pissing.

DANIELLE. Yep. Look Steph, a lovely, big, yellow, steaming, stream. Flowing out of me onto all your important documents. Ahhhhh. Squishy.

CHLOE. Everyone's watching, mouths open, looking dozy as fuck, as Dan squishes the piss into the papers. Smooshing it all into one big pissy mess. I'm just standing here – she's a fucking Goddess.

DANIELLE. You look a bit livid, Stephanie.

STEPHANIE. Livid.

DANIELLE. I am a fucking Amazonian Queen. I am the woman who pisses when she is pissed on. I am barefoot and knicker-less and I own this fucking moment.

STEPHANIE. No, you don't. Now, get the fuck out of my office.

Beat.

DANIELLE. We do.

CHLOE. Really fast.

DANIELLE. Oh my god.

CHLOE. That was amazing, Dan. You just did a wee on her desk – like proper on her desk – a big wee too.

DANIELLE. I drunk loads of Lucozade this morning.

CHLOE. She was so angry.

DANIELLE. Yeah. I can't believe I just did that. I don't know what happened to me I just – it just felt the right thing, y'know?

CHLOE. Yeah.

DANIELLE. Shit, I feel good.

CHLOE. I've got the tingles. Look.

DANIELLE. I just did that.

CHLOE. Yeah.

DANIELLE. Fuck me.

CHLOE. You just got your own back.

DANIELLE. I'm like Dave Benson-fucking-Phillips.

CHLOE. But with piss not gunge.

DANIELLE. Yeah.

CHLOE. Yeah.

DANIELLE. This is great.

CHLOE. I love you.

DANIELLE. Love you too.

What would Dave Benson-Phillips Do?

Revenge feels good
Revenge is sweet
Revenge makes me dizzy
My head feels full
It's cramped in my skull
With all the things I could do to you

You call me a whore 'cos I disagree with you?
I'll go in for a lick and bite down on your dick
You say I ain't smart enough and laugh in my face
I smash your head on your desk 'til your face is a mess
Don't think that I won't come get you
I remember what you did, what you say, what you do
I'm coming for you, we're coming for you

As Dave Benson-Phillips would declare
It feels good to get your own back
Hell yeah

Revenge is love
Revenge is pleasure
Revenge makes me tingle
My head feels full
It's cramped in my skull
With all the things I will do to you
With all the things I will do to you

As Dave Benson-Phillips would declare
It feels good to get your own back
Hell yeah

SCENE 3

CHLOE. I feel like a delinquent.

DANIELLE. We are delinquents, that's how everyone sees us. Sexy delinquents.

CHLOE. Yeah. Wandering the sexy streets of Hull.

DANIELLE. Might as well embrace it.

CHLOE. I feel all jibblies.

DANIELLE. Not a word Chlo.

CHLOE. I wanna bite your nose off.

DANIELLE. Calm down, people are starting to stare.

CHLOE. I can't.

DANIELLE. I love / you.

CHLOE. I love you.

DANIELLE. You little weirdo.

CHLOE. I aren't the only weirdo, you little weirdo. And I thought we didn't care if people stare? Delinquents?

DANIELLE. True. Feels good, right?

CHLOE. Aha, powerful.

DANIELLE. Told you this would put it all right.

CHLOE. And that's when it happened – I mean not literally right then but it was like pretty soon after that, but we don't want to make you wait 'cos that'll just be boring. 'Cos not much happened before this bit, and I know we said we'd try and tell the truth but no one wants to hear about how my Nan thinks her dead cat is haunting her or about Dan eating five Bird's Eye Potato Waffles yesterday or about how maybe we should get matching tattoos, not big ones little ones, classy as fuck / or…

DANIELLE. Chlo?

CHLOE. Right. Sorry. Boring.

DANIELLE. Round the corner come /

CHLOE. Two men.

DANIELLE. Too close.

CHLOE. 'Alright, gorgeous?'

DANIELLE. 'Fuck me, you're fit.'

CHLOE. 'You wanna suck my cock, beautiful?'

DANIELLE. Shit.

CHLOE. Leave it.

DANIELLE. No.

CHLOE. Maybe they're just trying to be nice.

DANIELLE. Seriously?

CHLOE. No.

DANIELLE. It's not a compliment, Chloe, they fucking know it's not a compliment.

CHLOE. I know.

DANIELLE. I can't just leave it. Not now, not after – I feel a bubbling anger in my tummy and I just need to get it out. I want to scream at them, shout real loud so everyone hears me, make myself just as big as them, all scary and…big.

(Small and disappointingly insignificant.) Fuck off.

CHLOE. 'What? How fucking dare you, you fucking ugly slags.' 'How dare you fucking talk to us like that, you fucking whore.' 'Know your fucking place you fat cow.'

DANIELLE. Shit.

CHLOE. Danielle.

DANIELLE. They loom over us.

CHLOE. I didn't realise they were so big.

DANIELLE. It's like, 'We are men, you are women. We are big, you are small. We have dicks, you have vaginas.'

CHLOE. And – shit, yeah, we do.

DANIELLE. And if dicks want to go somewhere /

CHLOE. Vaginas find it tough to stop them.

DANIELLE. And ours are feeling pretty insignificant right now.

CHLOE. Puny.

DANIELLE. Powerless.

CHLOE. Pathetic.

DANIELLE. Which sucks.

   Beat.

CHLOE. But it's different this time, it's got to be, hasn't it?

DANIELLE. They swagger away from us, fucking smug now they've put two irrelevant whores in their places. Things are right, it's all fair and balanced again.

CHLOE. But not for us.

DANIELLE. No, not for us.

CHLOE. Can we do something, Dan?

DANIELLE. Like what?

CHLOE. I dunno but – we wrote a list. We sang a song about Dave Benson-Phillips. There's got to be something.

   Beat.

Dan?

DANIELLE. What?

CHLOE. Guess where I am in my cycle.

DANIELLE. What? No.

CHLOE. Just do it.

DANIELLE. I don't know, day 9?

CHLOE. No. Day 15. You know what that means? I'm ovulating. Get it?

DANIELLE. No.

CHLOE. Oh, Dan, Dan, Dan. You're not thinking. What happens when a woman ovulates?

DANIELLE. I don't know.

CHLOE. She gets loads of discharge.

CHLOE puts her hand in her knickers, wipes herself and pulls her hand out and looks at it.

DANIELLE. What are you doing? Chloe – shit. And my strange little friend does the coolest fucking thing I've ever seen.

CHLOE. I'm running down the road after the men, I'm not very fast but they're only walking /

DANIELLE. She's actually fucking charging at them, I bet it looks pretty scary.

CHLOE. Oi! They turn round, they look a bit dozy and confused to see me standing right behind them.

MAN. What the /

CHLOE. I grab one of their heads – I think it was the one that called Dan a whore – and I smother it with my lady juice. I rub my hand up and down his smug-twat face like I'm giving him a facial. He grabs my wrist and glares at me. *(Beat.)* Ouch, fuck off. The hatred in his eyes is as painful as the Chinese burn on my skin. I know that look. I squiggle-wiggle free and pelt it back to Dan.

DANIELLE. And we run /

CHLOE. Like we've never run before. We run.

DANIELLE. Those cocks don't even know what's happened. Welcome to feminism.

CHLOE. Oh my god. I can't believe I just did that.

DANIELLE. Yeah, you did. I'm so proud of you, Chloe – fuck, so proud.

CHLOE. I don't know, I – look, Dan, I'm shaking.

DANIELLE. They didn't even know what was happening, stupid fucks.

CHLOE. I think I want to cry.

DANIELLE. Though, it probably won't stop them doing exactly the same again.

CHLOE. Dan?

DANIELLE. I think we need to start thinking bigger, being a bit more clever, you know?

CHLOE. Dan.

DANIELLE. Make them really regret what they did, make them change.

CHLOE. Danielle.

DANIELLE. What?

CHLOE. I don't feel good.

DANIELLE. What do you mean?

CHLOE. I think I'm gonna be sick.

DANIELLE. Bloody hell, Chloe. You do one thing – one fucking cool thing actually, and you feel sick?

CHLOE. Sorry.

DANIELLE. You need to calm down. Just try and go with the flow and – and think less. Yeah? You think too much.

CHLOE. Yeah.

DANIELLE. We've agreed to do this together, you and me, like always. Just us two against the world. Right?

CHLOE. Yeah.

DANIELLE. Good.

    Beat.

DANIELLE. You okay?

CHLOE. Yeah, it's just – just that look he gave me, people always look at me like I'm a freak / *(Beat.)* Grace would look at me like that.

DANIELLE. I s'pose that's what comes with being a feminist.

    Beat.

CHLOE. Yeah. *(Beat.)* She does feel powerful now. Like a tiger.

DANIELLE. Exactly. Like a fierce, fucking, tiger. *(Beat.)* I promise you Chloe, once we've finished this, once we've sorted it all out, you'll feel better. It'll be easier if we just keep going, it's when you stop and think that things start to feel scary and overwhelming. Trust me, we need to finish and then we'll be great, I promise. You trust me?

CHLOE. Always.

SCENE 4

CHLOE. We're carryin' on.

DANIELLE. We agree that it's best to / just

CHLOE. Carry on, yeah.

DANIELLE. This is fun.

CHLOE. Yeah, this is fun.

DANIELLE. Good. I drag my finger down the list and land on…

CHLOE. Jamie.

DANIELLE. Jamie.

CHLOE. Jamie, the controlling, condescending /

DANIELLE. Big word.

CHLOE. Twat. Thanks.

DANIELLE. Me and Jamie were /

CHLOE. Fuckin'. Love makin'. Sexin'. Doing the naked hokey cokey.

CHLOE sings a little of the hokey cokey in a 'sexy' way.

(Singing.) In, out, in, out. He shakes it all about.

DANIELLE. It was nice, to start. He'd make my womb do that little wave thing it does, y'know like, whoooa.

CHLOE. I love that feeling, all jumblies.

DANIELLE. Right. But then he started giving me 'advice'.

CHLOE. Advising her on what to wear.

DANIELLE. Guiding me through what to say.

CHLOE. Supervising her day.

DANIELLE. Managing my thoughts.

CHLOE. It was very kind of him to give up so much of his time to Dan's improvement.

DANIELLE. I was very grateful for his expertise. 'Cos you see, I was never really his kind of people, he was doing me a service really.

CHLOE. I hate him.

DANIELLE. But I couldn't be bothered with self-improvement. I like swearin' and being gross and havin' sex. I'm not a lady and no one is ever gonna make me into one.

CHLOE. So, Dan stopped fucking him and everything went back to normal. In other words, he got away with it, all of it, and I hate that.

DANIELLE. Until now, Chlo.

CHLOE. Yeah until now.

Beat.

DANIELLE. We've got a lovely little bit of revenge for him. A nice big shitty sandwich bag, full of shit, for the big bag of shit that he is.

The thing about Shitty Sandwich Bags

They're that Value brand, from Tesco
They're shitty and weak, prone to split and leak
No good for your tuna mayo.
If you accidently drop your shitty bag from a height
It will break.
If you swing it round your head real fast and let go
It will cover that wall or person in your tuna mayo.

Not much use for a shitty sandwich bag.
Who would ever use a shitty sandwich bag?
No one wants a shitty sandwich bag.

Unless you fill it with something nasty
Something yucky and dastardly
Something messy and gross
To fling at that person you hate the most

Tuna mayo just doesn't quite cut it
Best fill it with shit
Now it's a weapon, our dirty protest.

Always a use for a shitty sandwich bag.
Everyone can use a shitty sandwich bag.
Full to burst, my shitty sandwich bag.

DANIELLE. Ready, Chlo?

CHLOE. Ready.

CHLOE gets herself ready to be JAMIE.

DANIELLE. Cottingham, 5 o'clock. Chloe has, in her backpack, the sandwich bag full of shit. My shit.

CHLOE. It's not that gross.

DANIELLE. We find the church hall. The plan is to find Jamie, give him our little gift and leg it out of there.

CHLOE. It's *her* shit.

DANIELLE. But the second we walk through the door…

JAMIE. Dan – Danielle?

DANIELLE. Jamie. Hi. Fuck.

JAMIE. Hi? Sorry, I – what are you doing here? Did someone invite you? I…

DANIELLE. No. No. We're just here for a drink, we're just – we're out.

JAMIE. In Cottingham?

DANIELLE. Yep.

JAMIE. In the church hall?

DANIELLE. Yeah.

JAMIE. Right. Thing is, it's sort of a private party. My Grandad's birthday. *(Beat.)* You know what, it's fine.

DANIELLE. Oh right, sorry, we didn't know. *(To audience.)* We did. It was on Facebook. Jamie really needs to address his privacy settings.

JAMIE. Okay, sure.

DANIELLE. No, Jamie, we didn't know. Look, we can just /

JAMIE. Danielle, look it's probably a good thing you're here actually, I have something I've been meaning to tell you, I – fuck this is hard. Okay, right, okay – I'm sorry but I'm not sure we're in the same place.

DANIELLE. What?

JAMIE. I – shit why is this so hard?

DANIELLE. No idea.

JAMIE. Don't be angry with me, Danny. You're a fucking incredible person, I just – I fucked up.

DANIELLE. Oh my god, he's going to apologise.

JAMIE. Shit, I am such a cunt.

DANIELLE. Yeah, yeah, he is. Bloody hell.

JAMIE. Okay, look, I've met someone else.

DANIELLE. What? No, that's not…

JAMIE. It's serious. That's why I've gone underground recently. I wasn't sure how to – I wasn't sure how to tell you.

DANIELLE. Jamie, I ended it with you, I stopped calling you.

JAMIE. Okay, sure.

DANIELLE. Don't do that.

JAMIE. Look, I know this is shit for you /

DANIELLE. No.

JAMIE. And that it will hurt for a while /

DANIELLE. Doubt it.

JAMIE. But I think this could make you a stronger person.
Maybe the next bloke will treat you better, treat you like a
princess. You know Dan, I wish you'd stood up to me a bit
more, sort of laid down the law, I think I might not have
wandered if you had. Look, I'm not blaming you for how I
behaved or anything but you sort of give off the impression
that it's okay to sleep with you and not call or whatever.

DANIELLE. Yeah.

JAMIE. And when a man is a bit of a player, like me, we just
can't help ourselves when someone else comes along, you
know, if the woman you're with is a bit weak-willed.

DANIELLE. Are you fucking kidding me?

JAMIE. Millie really challenges me. She doesn't let me get
away with anything, I love that about her. *(Beat.)* Can I give
you some advice?

DANIELLE. Fuck no.

JAMIE. Men don't actually like it when you let us do everything
we want, a little discipline does us good. That's what Millie
says. Fucking hell, Danny I just – she's just incredible. I really
hope you find what I have with her. I hope you'll be able to
find your lover too.

DANIELLE. Lover?

JAMIE. Yeah. Lover. Knight in shining armour. Someone to
whisk you into his arms and keep you safe. A protector.

DANIELLE. That's gross.

JAMIE. I think it's probably about respect. I think you need
to respect yourself and then men might respect you a bit more.
Look, I don't want to tell you what to do /

DANIELLE. So, don't.

JAMIE. But, maybe if you didn't sleep with people quite so quickly you'd be able to make a real connection. That's what Millie did with me. She made me wait and – well I fell in love and then sex wasn't just sex. It was beautiful. You and me, it was never going to work out, I mean you slept with me the first time we met.

DANIELLE. Yeah, 'cos I wanted to. Jamie, I'm okay with sex being just sex. I like that. I'm not wounded. I'm / fine.

JAMIE. Shhh, shhh, shhh, shhhh. It's okay, it's okay.

DANIELLE. Suddenly, all these people are looking at me. All wearing the same pitying, empathy-dripping expressions. 'That's the girl that Jamie hurt.'

CHLOE. 'She's the one that he totally fucked over.'

DANIELLE. 'He broke her heart, poor love.'

CHLOE. 'Poor girl.'

DANIELLE. 'Poor sausage.'

CHLOE. 'Jamie's such a player.'

DANIELLE. 'He used her.'

CHLOE. 'He got what he wanted from her and just spat her out.'

DANIELLE. 'Although, she probably should have had a bit more self-respect.'

CHLOE. 'A bit more self-worth.'

DANIELLE. 'She'll never form lasting relationships by being a slag.'

CHLOE. 'Silly slapper.'

DANIELLE. 'Naïve whore.'

CHLOE. 'Poor slut.'

DANIELLE. All their faces are looking at me.

CHLOE. They really were.

DANIELLE. I feel all hot, like I'm proper burning up. There's hotness in my eyes and it's stinging and hot and wet and hot and –

JAMIE. I get it, oh Danny, Danny, no, no, don't cry.

DANIELLE. I'm not crying.

JAMIE. You've got tears in your eyes.

DANIELLE. They're drops of anger.

JAMIE. Look, let me just sort some stuff out and then maybe we could go get a drink, just the two of us and we can talk a bit more. I want to make it okay between us Danny, I think I can really help you, you know like I used to when we were going out. Give you some advice, about relationships and – everything really. If that's alright with… Claire?

CHLOE. Chloe.

DANIELLE. Mmm.

JAMIE. Great. Wait here. I'll be right back. And Danny?

DANIELLE. Yeah.

JAMIE. Chin up, we'll get you sorted.

DANIELLE. Shit.

CHLOE. What a fucker. Also, he does know my name – I'm your best friend. That's just – I hate it when people do that. You're not actually going to leave me here, are you, Dan? Not really?

DANIELLE. No. I'm not actually going to leave you.

CHLOE. Okay. Good.

DANIELLE. How the fuck has he done it again. We were meant to come here and make him pay for trying to 'improve' me and now he's just made me out to be fucking heartbroken. I ended it with him.

CHLOE. I know.

DANIELLE. I got myself out, Chlo. He hasn't fucked me over by sleeping with someone else.

CHLOE. I know.

DANIELLE. He thinks I'm weak, Chlo. He thinks I'm a little delicate flower that he's stamped on. He can fuck who he wants. Why the fuck would I give a shit? I don't. I don't care about him – I don't – fuck he's made me feel like I'm all damaged.

CHLOE. No cunt can shit on you, Dan.

DANIELLE. No.

CHLOE. But you can shit on them. Stick to the plan. He deserves it more than ever now.

The thing about shitty sandwich bags – Reprise

> Always a use for a shitty sandwich bag.
> Everyone can use a shitty sandwich bag.
> Full to burst, my shitty sandwich bag.

DANIELLE. Okay, pass it me.

CHLOE. Quick, he's coming back. Do it before he gets too close so you can really lob it, give it some power. Actually, let me just rip it a little – just to make sure.

DANIELLE. I pull my arm back, and overarm throw the shitty bag right at his head. It smacks into his forehead, it's a really good shot. The shit explodes over his face, the shitty bag sort of hangs off his nose. He's got some in his eyes /

CHLOE. Don't rub them, you'll get pink eye – oh, too late.

DANIELLE. He stands there – just still, like a fucking moron. Everyone's staring at him. It's silent. That's for being condescending, Jamie, and controlling, and a cunt. You think you hurt me but you didn't. I just got bored of you trying to make me into your vision of a woman. I don't want to be your kind of woman, Jamie, I'm my kind of woman. A woman who throws her own shit.

CHLOE. And we run – again. That was so good. Dan, you were amazing.

DANIELLE. Was I?

CHLOE. Yeah.

Pause.

What's up?

DANIELLE. Nothing.

CHLOE. It's okay to feel weird.

DANIELLE. Right, thanks.

CHLOE. No, Dan, I just mean, don't beat yourself up for not feeling the right things. I never feel the right things.

DANIELLE. Yeah.

CHLOE. Maybe it's like you said, we have to finish before we feel it.

DANIELLE. Right.

Pause.

CHLOE. Dan?

DANIELLE. I'm fine.

Beat.

CHLOE. Let's stop.

DANIELLE. What?

CHLOE. Let's just stop now, no one will know that we've given up, we'll just stop and pretend like we never made a list. We'll figure something else out. We'll make it all okay. I don't want to see you like this, I don't like it.

DANIELLE. We can't stop.

CHLOE. Why not?

DANIELLE. Because – what's the alternative? Going back to how we felt before?

CHLOE. Maybe it wasn't as bad as you think it was? I'm happy, whenever I'm with you, I'm happy. Let's just do stuff that makes us happy and forget everything else.

DANIELLE. It's not enough, nothing is ever enough. I need to do this. It'll be better.

CHLOE. And if it's not?

DANIELLE. Don't say that.

Beat.

Please don't ask me to stop, I can't – I need to finish this. Please, Chloe.

CHLOE. Okay.

Pause.

They both stop and come out of the moment.

CHLOE. You probably should have listened to me, Danielle.

DANIELLE. Yep, probably.

SCENE 5

DANIELLE. Come here.

They hug.

DANIELLE. Not too much more. Let's do a fun bit.

CHLOE. Yeah?

DANIELLE. We leave Jamie with shit on his face.

CHLOE. And we head back home to Hull, and we get shit-faced.

DANIELLE. Nice.

CHLOE. We sit on my bed and mix our drinks like we did when we were fourteen.

DANIELLE. Tequila, gin, beer, rum, gin, tequila, tequila, tequila, tequila, tequila /

CHLOE. Makes me happy. Danielle?

DANIELLE. Chloe.

CHLOE. Danielle.

DANIELLE. Chloe.

CHLOE. Danielle.

DANIELLE. Chloe, do you love me?

CHLOE. Yes. Yes, I love you. I love you and love you and love you.

Beat.

DANIELLE. Is that it?

CHLOE. What?

DANIELLE. That's not what you said.

CHLOE. Yeah it is.

DANIELLE. No, it's not.

Pause.

DANIELLE. Say it.

CHLOE. No.

DANIELLE. Say it.

CHLOE. Do I have to?

DANIELLE. We promised them we'd tell the truth.

CHLOE. *(Reluctantly.)* I love you so much, I sometimes wish I was a – penis /

DANIELLE. Big and / shiny.

CHLOE. Big and shiny, so that I could be inside you. That's how much I love you.

Beat.

CHLOE. I was fucked. I don't want to be a penis.

DANIELLE. It's the sentiment, right?

CHLOE. Yeah.

Beat.

Can I carry on now, please?

DANIELLE *shrugs.*

Beat.

Do you love me?

DANIELLE. Yes.

CHLOE. How much?

DANIELLE. So much that I want to just get your little twiggy arm and break it – snap.

CHLOE. I'm gonna bite your nose off.

DANIELLE. I'm gonna break your arm.

CHLOE. You'll have to catch me first, I'm a wily fucker.

CHLOE and DANIELLE start trying to catch each other.

DANIELLE. Stop moving / you little

CHLOE. Keep your face still / ow – stop shaking it

DANIELLE. That was your fault.

CHLOE. Will. You. Stay. Where / I. Put. You.

DANIELLE. Nope.

CHLOE jumps onto DANIELLE's front, wrapping her legs and arms around DANIELLE so that her arms are pinned to her side. DANIELLE frantically tries to throw her off but CHLOE is strong and clings on tighter. It gets more and more rough and less fun. Then all of a sudden they stop and calm down.

CHLOE. Tighter than tighter than tighter than tighter than tight.

DANIELLE. Tequila.

CHLOE slides down DANIELLE's legs onto the floor.

CHLOE. You're my best friend Dan, I don't need anyone else but you, ever. I'm so happy, now, here, I don't need anything else or anything really – no I don't – that's nice isn't it, Dan? If I died right now I'd be okay with it, long as you died too, 'cos I'm so happy. We'd float away and everything would be just lovely.

DANIELLE. You're talking crap, Chloe.

CHLOE. I'm not.

DANIELLE. You are. But yeah, yeah it would be nice.

CHLOE. Lovely.

DANIELLE. If only the world happened like it does in your head, we'd be sorted.

CHLOE. Happy.

DANIELLE. Happy.

CHLOE. N'night.

DANIELLE. Night.

CHLOE. Should I tell them about what happened when we were eight now?

DANIELLE. Yeah, I think you should.

CHLOE. Okay, so – right, okay. Remember earlier, right at the start, when Dan went /

DANIELLE. 'We're eight and things go a bit – pooey, for a few years.'

CHLOE. Yeah. Well, what happened was, at the start of year four our teacher / Mrs…

DANIELLE. Mrs. Sumner /

CHLOE. Danielle.

DANIELLE. Sorry.

CHLOE. Mrs. Sumner, decided we should be put in different classes, have opposite sittings at dinner and be 'encouraged' to play separately at break. It was for our own good, apparently we were too dependent on each other. So, at home time, my dad and Dan's mum, waited for us by the gate but – not near each other anymore. There was no, 'can Chloe come round for tea?' No knocking on. There was nothing. Danielle made new friends pretty quick, Amy and Lucy and Katie – you never used to like Katie but – you seemed to like each other now. I played with people, mostly the big games – bulldog, tig, the epic game of Peter Pan that included like forty kids, across like four different years, that went on for about four months. I got to play an Indian, once or twice I was Tiger Lily but most of the time I was just an unnamed. I liked to call myself Hiawatha, I didn't know that he was a man, it was before *Pocahontas* came out. Danielle played too sometimes, she was mostly a mermaid.

Things were sort of okay at primary, I mean – no, not good but – well it wasn't too bad either. It was familiar and – safe. When we moved up, when we went into year seven and

44

changed schools and had to get the bus and had to wear
uniform and had to use a locker instead of a drawer, that's
when it all went – that's when I struggled. I'm not good with
change. There was this girl – I don't know, I think – yeah,
I think some people can sense weakness, like they can sort
of smell it or something. I must of proper reeked. This girl,
Grace, she sniffed me out. I've never been normal, I know
no one is but most people are good at pretending they are. I
can't even do that. Danielle says that being different is better
than being normal, it means you're special but at eleven I
didn't want to be special, all I wanted was to be invisible –
which now I come to think of it is special, I suppose. I wanted
to be one of these people that no one notices, to be on the
periphery, never quite there. But I couldn't even do that
right. I was always in the way, always there for a quick shove
or a cheeky punch. Always there for a slap. I'd be shunned
and ignored but still plenty visible for a sneaky Fila heel to
the shin. Grace started a petition, the 'Chloe English should
be put down' petition. It got eighty-two signatures. I know,
it was sellotaped to my backpack. I stopped eating, stopped
sleeping, stopped washing. I got this huge, fuck-off cold sore
on my cheek, right here. Size of a two-pee coin. Cold sores
are face herpes, most people get them on their lips but my
dad kissed my cheek when I was a baby, when he had one on
his lip, so now I get them on my cheek and on my nose too
weirdly. Like Rudolph. So, I had this horrible, red, weeping
fucker on my cheek because I was stressed and run down and
I smelt and I was greasy and Danielle saw. She finally saw me,
and she understood. She was my friend again. She stopped
talking to anyone else. She never left my side. She wasn't
exactly my protector, you weren't cool enough to stop Grace
but she was a buffer. It happened less when she was there.
Mostly though, it was just such a relief to have her back. For
you to be mine again. I promised myself that I would never
let her go, and I haven't.

SCENE 7

DANIELLE. I wake up first, head pounding /

CHLOE. No, I was already awake, just had my eyes closed.

DANIELLE. Oh, right. I feel shit, proper, I-might-die-if-I-move-my-head, shit.

CHLOE. I feel fine.

DANIELLE. We don't have time to lay about and nurse my hangover, I pop three paracetamol and we get to work. Next up, Mrs. Sumner.

CHLOE. For separating us in year four.

DANIELLE. Revenge – to lock her in the boot of my car and leave her alone for six to eight hours.

CHLOE. I love this plan.

DANIELLE. But it didn't happen like that.

CHLOE. We look online to try and find her address, so we can kidnap her, and we realise we're gonna have to rethink it.

DANIELLE. Fuck.

CHLOE. What do we do now?

DANIELLE. Fucking typical.

CHLOE. Dan?

DANIELLE. I dunno. Fuck.

CHLOE. I was really looking forward to kidnappin' her.

DANIELLE. Me too.

   Beat.

Fuck it, let's just go to her house and see what happens. I'm not letting her get away with it just 'cos of this little – change in circumstance.

CHLOE. Really?

DANIELLE. Why not?

CHLOE. So we do. We slip on something sexy and make our way across Hull.

DANIELLE. Chloe lightens the mood with a little game.

CHLOE. Dead. Death. Dandruff.

DANIELLE. We're on Victoria Avenue.

CHLOE. Dementia.

DANIELLE. She's naming D words.

CHLOE. No, that's not – it's not just D words it's – look,
I'm saying that there are loads of bad or – loads of negative words
that start with D. So, Danielle, not one of them by the way /

DANIELLE. Cheers.

CHLOE. Is making me name them. I'm doing pretty well.
Dysentery. Dystopia. Danger.

DANIELLE. Daisies. Doughnuts / Desserts.

CHLOE. No, no, that's not… *(Pause.)* Dentists. Dairy / Debt.

DANIELLE. You can't have that one.

CHLOE. Lactose intolerance.

DANIELLE. Fine.

CHLOE. Which gives you – Diarrhoea.

DANIELLE. Nice.

CHLOE. Thanks. Devil. Demons. Dicks.

DANIELLE. I hate those cunts.

CHLOE. Dicks are way worse than cunts. Cunts are lovely.

DANIELLE. You'd know. What number is it again?

CHLOE. 128. There. Oh, no balloons.

DANIELLE. Why the fuck would there be balloons, Chloe?

CHLOE. So you know which house it is?

DANIELLE. It's not a four-year-old's birthday party.

CHLOE. No, I know.

DANIELLE. Ready?

CHLOE. Ready.

DANIELLE. We step into number 128, no one notices us.

CHLOE. There's a lot of black people here.

DANIELLE. White people dressed in black is what she means – this is Hull. Then the crowd parts a bit and we have a clear view. There. She's there. See?

CHLOE. Yeah. Mrs. Sumner.

DANIELLE. The bitch. She's in the back room, sort of tucked into a corner.

CHLOE. She's dead. Her husband /

DANIELLE. Catholic.

CHLOE. Wanted the lid off.

DANIELLE. An open coffin. Which means we can look at her.

CHLOE. Not in the eye though, they'll be closed otherwise it freaks people out.

DANIELLE. Come on.

CHLOE. No one's even looking at us, Dan.

DANIELLE. They're not looking directly, but that's only 'cos two young women in mourning clothes is the sexist thing they've ever seen, and it's not appropriate to get a boner at a wake.

CHLOE. We do look good. Sad sexy.

DANIELLE. Funeral sexy.

Funeral Sexy

Dressed all in black they boss the room
Sad faces quiver just for a second
With the sexy possibility that stalks towards them
Two dark angels smile and beckon
They ooze potential, a life to lead
A better way now his wife is dead

Funeral chic
Funereal power
Funeral sexy
This is what death should be

The dead are watching their envy grows
Two dark angels stalk the room
The dead can't touch but the living can
Moist red pouting lips are parting
They offer life, they offer hope
A warm vagina now his wife is dead

Funeral lust
Funereal power
Funeral sexy
This is what death should be
This is what death should be
This is what death should be
Funeral sexy.

DANIELLE. We have her to ourselves.

CHLOE. She looks thin.

DANIELLE. Fucking cow.

CHLOE. Can I touch? I want to touch her.

She slowly and deliberately traces around where her face would be.

Nice.

DANIELLE. It's us Mrs. Sumner. Danielle Lloyd and Chloe English. You remember yeah? Year four, you had a little meeting? It was with all the 'significant adults' in our lives, to discuss our 'unhealthy co-dependence' on each other, ring a bell?

CHLOE. You told my dad that it was 'unnatural for a girl of eight to rely so intensely on someone else, let alone a fellow eight-year-old.' My mum had just died, you fucking bitch.

DANIELLE. 'The girls should be separated to avoid a debilitating social anxiety in the future.'

CHLOE. 'The greatest kindness would be to remove the girls from each other's lives and let them flourish on their own.'

DANIELLE. Guess what Mrs. Sumner, we didn't flourish.

CHLOE. We withered.

DANIELLE. And died.

CHLOE. Just like you Mrs. Sumner.

DANIELLE. We didn't speak to each other for five years.

CHLOE. It was the worst five years of our lives.

DANIELLE. You destroyed two little girls.

CHLOE. It's a good fuckin' thing you're dead.

DANIELLE. 'Cos what we had planned would have been much worse.

CHLOE. I wanna do something, Dan. No point chucking her in the boot now though, is there?

DANIELLE. No.

CHLOE. No. She looks real peaceful doesn't she. Like, sort of nice and kind.

DANIELLE. Yeah, but we know better.

CHLOE. Yeah, we do. *(Beat.)* What if we give her a makeover?

DANIELLE. Okay?

CHLOE. Make her look like she really was, a spiteful, horrible, monster-person?

DANIELLE. Evil.

CHLOE. Like – like that scary old woman in *Robin Hood Prince of Thieves*.

DANIELLE. 'The painted man!' Shit, she terrified me.

CHLOE. Yeah.

DANIELLE. Or Chucky?

CHLOE. Yeah, she's already got the ginger hair.

DANIELLE. Right, give us your make-up.

CHLOE. Put black under her eyes, make her look dead.

DANIELLE. She is dead.

CHLOE. More dead.

DANIELLE. I'll do a creepy clown smile too.

CHLOE. Should I try and open her eyes?

DANIELLE. Fuck yes.

CHLOE. Black some of her teeth.

DANIELLE. Her jaw won't open.

CHLOE. And then /

DANIELLE. Out of bloody nowhere her husband is suddenly lurking right / behind…

MR. SUMNER. Hello. I'm John. You must be ex-students of Eve's?

DANIELLE. Yes.

MR. SUMNER. Well, it was so kind of you to come.

DANIELLE. Right.

MR. SUMNER. What's that?

DANIELLE. What?

MR. SUMNER. On her face…

DANIELLE. Nothing.

MR. SUMNER. Let me – what have you done to her face?

DANIELLE. We…

MR. SUMNER. You monsters. How could you? Do you have no compassion? No respect? How dare you? This is my wife – this is my wife – you can't – get out. Get out of my house. You are disgusting. Get out, now, before I call the police.

DANIELLE. We're not disgusting, you are. You married her. You're the one that fucked her.

MR. SUMNER. GET OUT.

DANIELLE. She made our lives hell. She fucking destroyed us.

CHLOE. Everyone's looking at us, Dan.

DANIELLE. You're all standing about thinking she was a fucking saint just 'cos she's dead and she wasn't. She was evil. Fucking evil. We were just making her look like her true self.

CHLOE. Dan.

DANIELLE. She deserves to be dead.

CHLOE. Please, Dan, can we go?

DANIELLE. I hope she rots in hell. Fuck you, Mrs. Sumner.

CHLOE. Dan please, I don't like it.

DANIELLE. FUCK YOU.

CHLOE. Come on Dan, come on. Sorry. We're sorry.

DANIELLE. Don't apologise Chloe. We're not fucking sorry.

CHLOE. Let's go, please let's just go. Come on. Sorry, we're sorry. We didn't – please, we just want to go. We're sorry.

CHLOE drags DANIELLE away.

Beat.

DANIELLE. What the fuck, Chloe?

CHLOE. What?

DANIELLE. Why didn't you back me up?

CHLOE. I did.

DANIELLE. No, you didn't. You stood there being all weak and – and fucking apologising. We're meant to be doing this together.

CHLOE. We are doing it together.

DANIELLE. Really?

CHLOE. I'm sorry – I just – he was so angry and – sad and I – it made me feel bad for him and – and it was pretty scary in there when everyone started staring and shouting at us. I think someone was calling the police. I wanted to go. I kept saying that, Dan – I just wanted to go. I think – I would have liked it if you'd listened to me. I needed to go, I needed you to come with me. I'm not good with stuff like that, you know that, Dan, you know and you / didn't…

DANIELLE. So, this is my fault? Y'know / for once it would have been nice if you'd stuck up for me, like I always do for you.

CHLOE. I'm not sayin' that. I'm just – I just think you should have listened to me, for once.

Beat.

Not always.

DANIELLE. What?

CHLOE. Not always.

DANIELLE. Yes, always.

CHLOE. Not with Grace.

DANIELLE. Oh, fuck off Chloe.

CHLOE. You're not always the best friend you think you are, sometimes you get it wrong.

DANIELLE. Yeah? Well maybe I can say the same about you.

CHLOE. I'm a great best friend.

DANIELLE. You're fucking exhausting, Chloe. Do you see that? This was meant to be something great for us – really fucking life-changing but you couldn't let it happen, you have to question everything. 'Are you sure, Dan? Maybe we shouldn't. I feel funny.' You've ruined this whole thing, Chloe. It was supposed to make everything better but you've shat on it and made it all worse. I needed you to be in this with me but instead you follow me round like a little lost puppy, always there but never any use. Always so fucking close, it makes my skin crawl – you touching and stroking, all the time. You think sometimes I get it wrong? What about all the fucking times I've had to put up with shit like that, all the times I've said nothing but really I just wanted you to fuck off. To leave me alone, to let me be me, even for just a couple of fucking hours. Maybe Mrs. Sumner was fucking right? Maybe we are better off alone. Because sometimes I hate being Danielle and Chloe. Sometimes, Chloe, you suffocate me. You're fucking suffocating me.

CHLOE. I can leave you alone, if you want. *(Pause.)* Do you want me to leave you alone?

DANIELLE. Yeah.

CHLOE. Okay. *(Beat.)* I love you Danielle.

CHLOE leaves.

DANIELLE. Fuck.

SCENE 8

Glued

DANIELLE: If you could glue yourself to me, you would
You'd pritt stick us together, if you could
As close as can be, nose to nose
All fingers touching and our toes

You scratch my skin when there's no itch
We're sewn together, stitch by stitch
Our skin is embroidered with each other's shit
I don't want you there, unpick it

I'm tired of being with you
I'm tired of you so near
Leave me alone my love
Leave me alone my dear

DANIELLE. I know what you're thinking, you like Chloe better. I like Chloe better. She's soft, like girls are s'posed to be. I'm not – no, that's not true, I am, I can be but it's hard. It's hard to be soft. God. You let your guard down a little too much, I let someone see all the guts and innards of me and they nod and smile but I know, I know they're not coming back. They've run for the fucking hills – which is quite a long way out of Hull, actually. I do get that I'm not easy to love. Never have been. It's meant to be impossible not to love a baby, right? Like physically they manipulate adults to love them, big eyes, big heads, so cute you could squish them up and swallow them whole. Not me. I'm not trying to make you feel sorry for me. *(Beat.)* Fuck it, no I *am* trying to make you feel sorry for me. It's not my fault that my mum couldn't love me, that she was so fucking young she hardly knew what was happening to her, that as her tummy grew she felt like she'd been taken over by an intruder. Little intruder me.
A little parasite that just got bigger and bigger and stronger until one day I squelched on out and looked up at her with those big manipulative eyes and she just… *(Pause.)* I tried to make it up to her. Tried so desperately to make it better, I think she tried too but it never worked. Then she met

her dream man, he's nice, they had four babies. Perfect, manipulative, babies. They had what I didn't. They managed just fine to get her attention, to make her love them. Poor little Danielle. *(Beat.)* But then I have Chloe. Chloe needs me, Chloe loves me like no one has ever loved anyone ever. She does this thing where she has to touch me, if I'm near, like just sitting on the sofa or walking or – whatever. If I'm close enough to touch then Chloe will. It's like she has to know I'm there, even when she can see me, she has to make sure I'm real. She's always been like that, even before her mum died I think. She used to do this thing, to her mum, where she'd grab that little bit of skin under her chin and rub it between her knuckles, like little pincers. She always complains that I'm not jowly enough, and she can't do it to her dad 'cos of his stubble – it's the softness. I think that might be one of the things she misses most about her mum. When we were fourteen – we'd only just become friends again – she started doing this thing where she'd pretend to be my pet monkey. It was when we were at the baths, we were in the pool and she'd climbed onto my front, wrapping herself all tight around me, and then she put her nose up to mine. The game was that I had to try and look away and she had to make sure I was always looking at her. So, if I turned my head she would do this little squeak and nose to nose she'd stare into my eyes, all intense. If I dunked us under the water, she'd just cling on tighter. If I spun round and round really fast she'd just squeak and squeal and press her cheek up to mine. It was pretty fucking adorable. She loves that game, being so close to me, it's – it's everything. I think if she could she'd be literally glued to me. My little limpet. *(Pause.)* She's never left me like this before. She's not good on her own. *(Long pause.)* She'll come back.

Glued (reprise)

DANIELLE: If you could glue yourself to me, you would
You'd pritt stick us together, if you could
As close as can be, nose to nose
All fingers touching and our toes

You scratch my skin when there's no itch
We're sewn together, stitch by stitch
Our skin is embroidered with each other's shit
So close together, a perfect fit

I need to be beside you
I need you so so near
Never leave me my love
I hate alone my dear

DANIELLE. Fuck.

DANIELLE exits.

SCENE 9

The stage/space is empty. CHLOE peaks her head out. She enters, tentatively, she looks at the bin bag. She hums 'Glued' to herself.

DANIELLE enters, she watches CHLOE for a long while.

DANIELLE. Hi.

CHLOE. Hi.

   Pause.

DANIELLE. I love / you.

CHLOE. I love you.

DANIELLE. I'm sorry.

CHLOE. No, it's okay.

DANIELLE. Yeah? You okay?

CHLOE. Yeah.

DANIELLE. I thought you'd left me forever.

CHLOE. No.

DANIELLE. Come here.

   They hug.

CHLOE. Tighter, than tighter, than tight.

DANIELLE. Always.

CHLOE. Yeah.

   Beat.

Dan?

DANIELLE. Mm?

CHLOE. I sorta wish we could finish here.

   They both look at the bin bag, then out at the audience.

DANIELLE. We promised.

CHLOE. I know.

They pull apart from their hug.

DANIELLE. Chloe was only away for a couple of hours.
Lots can happen in a couple of hours.

CHLOE. I'm not good on my own.

Pause.

DANIELLE. The bin bag.

*She goes over to the bin bag and tries to lift it, she isn't surprised
by how heavy it is. She rips a tiny hole in the bag and takes a tiny
peak. She recoils very slightly. She looks at CHLOE.*

DANIELLE. Chloe?

CHLOE. Do I have to?

DANIELLE. No one here's gonna judge you, Chlo.

CHLOE. Thanks Dan. Thanks everyone.

Long pause.

CHLOE. It's funny isn't it, how these things happen. I was just
curious, I wanted to see what she was like and whether I was
brave enough now, after everything we'd done, if I could face
up to her. I found out where she lived – earlier, when Dan
was preparing for Jamie, I just looked it up and there it was.
I didn't not tell Dan, I just – I didn't tell her, it's different.
At that point, I didn't think I'd do anything with it, I thought
I'd wimp out like always but Dan was being so brave and
doing all this great stuff that I thought maybe – maybe I
might pluck up the courage. And I did. After Dan said she
needed to be alone for a couple of hours – which I completely
understand by the way, I can be a bit suffocating.

DANIELLE. No.

CHLOE. It's okay, Dan, really. Well, I thought maybe a couple of hours is all I need to – to make things right between me and Grace. So, I went to her house. She didn't recognise me at first, smiled at me in a 'I'm not going to buy anything' sort of way, must have thought I was an Avon lady or Jehovah's Witness or something, but then I said, I'm Chloe English and her face sort of dropped. She invited me in. Grace Jones invited me into her house. She lives on her own, in this little flat, it's nice. She made me a cup of tea. We talked – no, she talked. She talked and talked and talked. Said how sorry she was, how her parents were going through a divorce when she was at school and that she took it out on me. That she wasn't making excuses but that it was really hard and – and that she was so sorry. She kept saying sorry, over and over. Sorry I hit you, sorry I made you cry, sorry I spat, sorry I kicked, sorry I made your life so shit. I didn't say anything. It wasn't helping. She was so nice, so apologetic and I could feel myself not hating her. She wanted to make it up to me somehow, she said it had haunted her too and she thought I was so brave for coming to see her, that she had wanted to find me for years but didn't have the guts. Everything I thought Grace was, what I thought she would be and she wasn't. She'd changed. She'd become nice – and kind and gentle. That wasn't fair. That's not fair, is it? 'Cos I was supposed to put her in her place, to rebalance it. I was supposed to be the one to take back control, to teach her a lesson, to do to her what she did to me. She'd taken that away from me, her being so nice had taken what I needed away. And I started to hate her again, 'cos she was ruining stuff, she was fucking it up for me all over again. I wouldn't let her get away with it this time, I'm not thirteen any more, I can take control, I can stand up for myself. I know that sounds so stupid / but I…

DANIELLE. No, it doesn't. She made your life hell. It's totally understandable, Chlo.

CHLOE. So, I…

DANIELLE. It's okay.

CHLOE. I say, I want another cup of tea. She walks into the kitchen and starts filling the kettle. I follow her. In the doorway, on the wall, she has a magnet, with knives. The tap's running so she can't hear me. She turns the tap off. I'm right behind her. I can see the little hairs on the back of her neck lifting up. We take a deep breath in. Then... She exhales. All the air comes out of her lungs, out, out, out. And then I do it again and again and again and again. Knife in, knife out, knife in, knife out, knife in, knife out. And then she just sorta – flops.

I didn't stay very long after. I'd already been nearly two hours and Dan said she only needed a couple of hours alone. So, I left – we left and came straight back here, to Dan.

Pause.

DANIELLE. All done?

CHLOE nods.

DANIELLE. Better?

CHLOE nods.

DANIELLE. I'm really proud of you, Chloe.

CHLOE. Thanks. What do we do with her now?

DANIELLE. No idea.

CHLOE. What do *we* do now?

DANIELLE shrugs.

I'm tired.

CHLOE. Me too.

DANIELLE. It might be nice to stop.

CHLOE. Nice to be still.

DANIELLE. Yeah.

CHLOE. Yeah.

Beat.

You're my best friend, Danielle.

DANIELLE. Even now?

CHLOE. Especially now.

DANIELLE. It didn't exactly go to plan.

CHLOE. No.

DANIELLE. Sorry.

CHLOE. No.

DANIELLE. Do you think I fucked you up?

CHLOE. No.

DANIELLE. I'm sorry.

CHLOE. No.

Beat.

Danielle?

DANIELLE. Chloe?

CHLOE. I think whatever happens next, we should just stay together – alone.

DANIELLE. Always.

<u>Her</u>

Yank my legs off and do me wrong
I've still got arms to pull me along
Kick my shin and punch my face
Try to isolate, I know my place

It's with her, right here
Always
Her, her, her
I'm with her, no fear
Always

Her, her, her

We come as a pair, two halves as one
With each other no harm can be done
'Til death parts us, for better or not
We'll stay together here, in this spot

I'm with her, right here
Always
Her, her, her
I'm with her, no fear
Always
Her, her, her

We're a bit punchy, naughty
But don't be all snooty and haughty
'Cos we have something that you need
Someone to die for, a love to bleed

I'm with her, right here
Always
Her, her, her
Stay with me, no fear
Always
Her, her, her

*DANIELLE takes CHLOE's hand and brings it up to under her chin.
CHLOE smiles, closes her eyes and very gently rubs DANIELLE's neck
with her knuckles. They exhale, together.*

END.

Maths Teacher's Bulge

Ellen Brammar

James Frewer

Trying to be Edgy ♩ = 128

Py-thag-o-ras, you tempt me, Oh hy-pot-en-use you minx Con, sin, tan, you troll-ops, A-cute an-gle? Why yes me thinks. The maths tea-cher's bulge is brew-ing, it lies quiet and dor mant no more, it's a-wo-ken by num-bers and fig-ures es-pec ia-lly my fig-ure I'm sure.

We Hate Them

Ellen Brammar

James Frewer

©JamesFrewer

What Would Dave Benson-Phillips Do?

Ellen Brammar

James Frewer

Shitty Sandwich Bag

Ellen Brammar

James Frewer

Funeral Sexy

Ellen Brammar

James Frewer

Glued

Ellen Brammar

James Frewer

If you could glue your-self to me you would, you'd pritt-stick us to - geth-er if you could. As

close as can be nose to nose all fin - gers touch-ing and our toes. You

scratch my skin when there's no itch. We're sewn to-geth-er stitch by stitch. Our

skin is em-broi-de-red with each oth-ers shit. I don't want you there un - pick it,___ I'm

tired of be - ing with you I'm so tired of you so near.

Leave me a - lone my love.   Leave me a - lone my dear.

Her

Ellen Brammar

James Frewer

www.ingramcontent.com/pod-product-compliance
Ingram Content Group UK Ltd.
Pitfield, Milton Keynes, MK11 3LW, UK
UKHW020707280225
455688UK00012B/305

9 781786 823649